The PAINTER & BRIDE

Eva Howarth

Salem House Publishers
Topsfield, Massachusetts

Created and produced by
PHOEBE PHILLIPS EDITIONS

Copyright © Phoebe Phillips Editions 1989

First published in the United States
by Salem House Publishers, 1989,
462 Boston Street, Topsfield, Massachusetts 01983

ISBN 0 88162 458 6

Design: Caroline Reeves
Typeset by J&L Composition Ltd
Colour origination by Columbia Offset
Printed in Italy by Rotolito Lombarda

Introduction to
The PAINTER and The BRIDE

A toast to our celebration of marriage, the ritual of weddings and the mystery of the Bride, portrayed throughout ten centuries of art and through the eyes of 22 famous painters, from Giotto and Van Eyck to Rembrandt and Grandma Moses!

Greek Vase Painting

Sixth century BC   British Museum, London

In ancient Greece the marriage ceremony was conducted in the home, not in a temple.

Before the marriage could take place the bride's father had to ask the permission and blessing of his household gods.

The bride's procession from one home to another followed. She would be dressed in white, her face covered by a veil, with a crown on her head. The nuptial torch was carried in front of her.

In addition to the bride's family and friends, there were often a number of heralds in the procession. These men performed a religious function, singing a sacred marriage chant.

When she reached her new home the bride would be met by her future husband. He would seize her with a pretence of force, while her women companions would make a show of defending her.

In the house further ceremonies were performed. All her life the bride would have prayed and sacrificed to her family's household gods. Now she would be introduced to a new domestic altar and made aware that in the future she would have to pray to other gods and look to them for protection.

She would be sprinkled with water and would touch the sacred fire while prayers were said. As a final symbolic act of unity the newly married husband and wife would share a cake.

The Aldobrandini Wedding

First century BC   Vatican Library, Rome

In AD 79 Mount Vesuvius erupted and totally buried the town of Pompeii in southern Italy. Excavations began in the eighteenth century, when a town in an astonishingly fine state of preservation emerged.

One of the works of art that came to light was a wall painting in a villa. The Aldobrandini Wedding is a section of this. It shows Venus, the goddess of love, talking to the young bride.

Roman girls often married at the age of twelve and boys at the age of fourteen. The marriages were usually arranged by the parents.

On her wedding day the bride would present her dolls and other toys to the household gods. She would then lay aside the kind of toga only worn by young girls.

For her wedding she would wear a long white tunic with a girdle tied round her waist with a special double knot, called the knot of Hercules.

Over her dress would be a yellow cloak, and she would have sandals of the same colour. On her hair would be a garland of myrtle and orange blossom and, over it, a transparent, flame-coloured veil.

Roman weddings were occasions for celebration, and the bride would be accompanied to her new home by musicians as well as friends and relations.

Many of the rituals are familiar to us today. The bride wore a ring and ate a special cake as part of the religious ceremony. She also had bridesmaids and was carried over the threshold of her new home. It was not the bridegroom who did this, but the best man.

Marriage at Cana
Giotto di Bondone
Italian c. 1267–1337   Arena Chapel, Padua

Giotto's *Marriage at Cana* is part of a series of frescoes in the Arena (or Scrovegni) Chapel in Padua. He was commissioned to carry out the work by a rich citizen of Padua named Enrico Scrovegni. By this act of patronage Scrovegni hoped to atone for the sins of his father, who was a notorious usurer at a time when the Church condemned usury as a sin.

This fresco illustrates one of the first miracles performed by Jesus. The wedding guests had no wine to drink, so Jesus ordered the servants to fill six stone pots with water and give one to the governor to try. On tasting, it was found that the water had been changed to wine.

Giotto enjoyed fame and success in his lifetime. The poets Petrarch and Boccaccio wrote sonnets about him, and Dante was a friend of his. Scrovegni's father, the usurer, appears in hell in Dante's *Divine Comedy*.

The Mystical Marriage of St Catherine
Master of Heiligenkreutz

German Early fifteenth century   Kunsthistoriches Museum, Vienna

According to legend, St Catherine, in a vision, was transported to Heaven by the Virgin Mary and was betrothed there to Christ.

In this painting, which depicts her mystical marriage, two other saints act as witnesses; they are St Dorothy and St Barbara.

St Catherine was reputed to be a beautiful maiden with many suitors. She refused all of them and remained faithful for the rest of her life to her vows.

The painting is a fine example of the International Gothic style. The figures are natural; details such as the crown of St Catherine, the headdresses of the other saints and their garments are all wholly realistic.

The women are tall and slender, with high foreheads and fine features. The hands are expressive and, in one departure from realism, the length of the fingers is greatly exaggerated.

The background is formed by part of a Gothic building.

St Catherine, who probably lived in the Roman Empire some centuries earlier, is nevertheless dressed in contemporary fashion. This was a common practice of medieval painters.

Its elegance and rich, jewel-like qualities made the International Gothic style popular in royal courts in a number of European countries.

The Arnolfini Wedding
Jan van Eyck
Netherlandish c.1390–1441   National Gallery, London

The young man in the painting is Giovanni Arnolfini, a rich Italian
merchant who had come to the Netherlands on business. The girl is
his bride, Jeanne de Chenany.

There is no priest present in the painting, but before the Council
of Trent in 1560 the presence of a priest was not altogether
obligatory.

Witnesses, however, were needed, and they can be seen reflected
in the mirror on the wall. One of them, who is dressed in blue, was
almost certainly van Eyck himself.

The picture is full of symbolism; one of the candles in the
chandelier is lit, even though it is broad daylight – a wedding candle
which represents the all-seeing eye of God. On top of the chair
behind the girl is a carving of St Margaret, the patron saint of
childbirth. Even the dog has a part to play, for he symbolizes the
wife's fidelity.

Up until that time it was still the practice of artists to paint with
powdered pigment mixed with liquid, most usually egg, to form a
paste.

Van Eyck had discovered that the use of oil instead of egg as a
binding agent gave him a superior kind of paint which enabled him
to produce wonderfully rich and deep colours. He was thus the
inventor of oil painting.

The Marriage of the Virgin
Jean Fouquet
French c.1420–c.1481   Musée Condé, Chantilly

The marriage of the Virgin Mary was a popular subject for medieval paintings.

According to the Bible, Mary told the High Priest of the Temple that she wished to remain a virgin all her life. But the priest, among others, heard a voice saying that all the unmarried men who belonged to the House of David should come to the temple altar and bring a staff.

A number of men came forward, including the young man who is so annoyed at not being successful that he has broken his staff. Another figure in the foreground, who is probably a rich merchant, is also angered by his rejection.

Joseph, on the other hand, was reluctant to come forward because he did not think it seemly that a man of his age should marry a young girl. But, as can be seen, his staff sprouted immediately as a sign that he was the bridegroom chosen by God.

Jean Fouquet was the most famous French painter of the fifteenth century. He specialized in miniatures and illuminated manuscripts. One of his patrons was Etienne Chevalier, the Lord High Treasurer of France, for whom he created a beautifully illustrated prayer book.

The Marriage of the Virgin is one of the paintings from that book. It has something of the appearance of a stage set, no doubt because the legend was so often the subject of mystery plays.

Princess Sibylle of Cleve as Bride
Lucas Cranach
German 1472–1553   Schlossmuseum, Weimar

Princess Sibylle of Cleve was fourteen years old when she became the bride of the Elector of Saxony, John Frederick, known as the Magnanimous.

In the picture she is dressed as the height of fashion demanded. She wears a red dress with slashed sleeves and bodice and heavy gold chains. Only privileged noblewomen at that time were allowed to wear red; women of lower rank were forbidden to wear bright colours and expensive materials.

The laws which dictated what could be worn were known as the sumptuary laws. They were in force in many parts of Europe and were used to control expenditure – much as bank rates are used today.

In some places they were extremely unpopular. When a peasant revolt broke out in sixteenth-century Germany, for instance, one of the rebels' demands was the repeal of some of the sumptuary laws.

The practice of slashing material and letting the lining show through the gaps in the fabric has a curious history. It originated from the soldiery, who cut fabric up and used the pieces to patch up their torn uniforms. The custom became known at the French court, where it was adopted as a fashion in the sixteenth century. Before long it spread over much of Europe.

Lucas Cranach was a court painter in Saxony for almost half a century. His painting of Princess Sibylle as a bride is signed, like a number of his paintings, with a winged snake followed by the initials LC.

The Peasant Wedding
Pieter Brueghel the Elder

Flemish c.1525–1569   Kunsthistorisches Museum, Vienna

The picture is so natural and has such an air of spontaneity that to look at it is to feel you are taking part in the wedding feast.

As in so many Brueghel paintings, each figure is a character study; the bride is the centre of interest, and she knows it.

Her expression is perhaps a little smug. No doubt a number of those shown are members of her family, and her parents, sitting on her left, have evidently done her proud.

The question to which no one has yet found the answer is: where is the bridegroom?

The feast would certainly take place in the home of the bride's parents, and, according to custom, the bridegroom would be expected to serve the bride. (After the wedding, of course, the bride would do the serving.) Perhaps the bridegroom is the young man who is passing dishes to those who are seated at the same table as he is.

No one has shown more clearly what comfortable Flemish peasant life was like, or depicted it with more zest, than the elder Brueghel.

Marriage of Maria de' Medici to Henry IV
Peter Paul Rubens
Flemish 1577–1640   Louvre, Paris

Maria de' Medici, as Queen Mother of France, commissioned Rubens to decorate the Luxembourg Palace, her residence in Paris. The work involved painting a cycle of twenty-four pictures illustrating the most important events in her life. This was a great honour, but it also gave rise to problems.

Maria de' Medici saw herself as the central figure in a glorious reign and expected Rubens to show this in his paintings. Her son, King Louis XIII, who continually quarrelled with his mother, had very different views on the subject and also required them to be reflected. Consequently, the question of what should be included was debated for months.

Rubens, a masterly painter, was very much a man of the world. He was a courtier, a diplomat and almost certainly a spy. With extraordinary artistic and diplomatic skill he succeeded in producing a cycle of paintings which satisfied all parties and delighted posterity.

One of the paintings was of Maria de' Medici's marriage to the future King Henry IV of France. Rubens had been present at this event as a young man.

The marriage, which took place in Italy, was by proxy. Such marriages were not uncommon among royal personages at a time when they often found it inconvenient to travel abroad.

The Jewish Wedding
Rembrandt Harmensz van Rijn

Dutch 1606–1669   Rijksmuseum, Amsterdam

This was one of the last pictures which Rembrandt painted.

The deep affection which the couple feel for each other is beautifully expressed. The colours are subtle and the man's golden sleeve, which latterday critics have so much admired, gives an almost magical quality to the painting.

Strangely, the picture was not much admired in Rembrandt's lifetime. He enjoyed considerable popularity in his younger days, but public taste changed, and he died a poor man.

There is a mystery about the title of this painting, and there are good reasons for believing that it did not represent a Jewish wedding at all. Jewish brides were traditionally dressed in white and wore white veils. Rembrandt lived in a street in Amsterdam where a number of his neighbours were Jewish, and he would certainly have been aware of their wedding customs.

The misleading title seems to have been given to the painting in England in the nineteenth century.

A Courtesan Dreaming of Her Wedding
Utamaro, Kitagawa
Japanese 1753–1806   British Museum, London

The training of a geisha girl sometimes began when she was only seven years old. Among the skills she was taught were music, dancing, singing, graceful behaviour and the intricacies of the tea ceremony.

Geishas were permitted, if they so wished, to find a patron, and sometimes the relationship led to marriage.

On her wedding day tradition demanded that the bride's face was completely covered in white make-up, to which eye-shadow and lipstick were added. Her hair was combed in an elaborate high style and stiffly lacquered. She was dressed in a kimono, which she wore only for her wedding, with an *obi* – a decorative broad belt.

Utamaro was one of the best-known Japanese painters and designers of his time. In Japan he was famous mainly for his landscapes and drawings of insects. In Europe he is better known for his designs for colour prints, many of them featuring women, some of whom were prostitutes and bath-house girls.

The Wedding
Francisco de Goya

Spanish 1746–1828   Prado Museum, Madrid

Goya, as court painter to King Charles IV of Spain, was commissioned to prepare a series of cartoons for the royal tapestry works.
The finished tapestries were to be hung in the King's study.

The Wedding is one of the greatest of the pictures in this series. It
is also a bitter attack on the practice of marrying for financial
convenience.

There was nothing new in this custom; it had been accepted for
centuries that marriages were arranged by the couple's parents. A
rich bridegroom was regarded by them, and indeed by most girls, as
the ideal marriage partner, though the girls often prayed that their
particular rich man should also be young and handsome.

In eighteenth-century Spain, however, the preference for a rich
bridegroom was sometimes carried to absurd lengths.

In Goya's picture the beautiful young bride is marrying a man who
is so ugly that he looks like a monkey. It is also clear from his clothes
that he is rich. It is easy to pick out the bridegroom's friends among
the wedding guests, for they are all old.

The women are looking at the bride not with pity, but rather with
a conspiratorial expression on their faces.

Goya painted many portraits of beautiful women in happier
circumstances, among them the so-called 'proud and beautiful
Duchess of Alba', the great romantic love of his life. On the subject
of marriage, however, it was his power as a satirist that was most in
evidence.

Fête at the Château de Versailles on the Occasion of the Marriage of the Dauphin in 1745
Eugéne-Louis Lami

French 1800–1890   Victoria and Albert Museum, London

The Dauphin was the eldest son of King Louis XV of France and the heir to his throne; his bride was Marie Joseph of Saxony. The Dauphin died in 1765, and it was his son who came to the throne five years later as King Louis XVI.

The painting shows Versailles at a time when French fashion set the tone for courts everywhere in Europe. The bride standing at the top of the staircase is dressed in a magnificent gown with a tight bodice and a very wide skirt extended sideways.

The men have powdered wigs, a strange and uncomfortable fashion which survived in France until the Revolution of 1789. It still lingers in England in the prescribed costume for judges, although the powder is less in evidence than it used to be. The ladies did not wear wigs, but did powder their hair.

Lami was a versatile artist who was much in vogue at the court of Napoleon III and the Empress Eugénie. A number of his paintings can be found at the Palace of Versailles today.

The Wedding of the Prince of Wales and Princess Alexandra
William Powell Frith

English 1819–1909   Royal Collection, London

The future King Edward VII of England and Princess Alexandra of Denmark were married in St George's Chapel, Windsor, in March 1863. It was a splendid occasion attended by royalty from many European countries.

The bride wore a white satin dress decorated with orange blossoms and myrtle and a long veil made of the finest English lace. Following royal tradition, she wore her veil off her face. Eight bridesmaids carried her train.

The Prince of Wales wore army uniform and the magnificent Garter robes.

Queen Victoria sat in one of the balconies. It was some fifteen months since her husband, the Prince Consort, had died, but she still regarded herself as being in full mourning, and she was dressed entirely in black.

Princess Alexandra caused some concern by arriving at the chapel nearly ten minutes late. To those who knew her well this was no surprise; to others it was a foretaste of what was to come.

She was easily forgiven for being late, for she was a beautiful girl, who was quickly taken to the heart of the British public.

Frith was a popular painter who recorded in painstaking detail events in Victorian and Edwardian Britain – most notably Derby day. He became a Royal Academician when a vacancy was created by the death of Turner.

Le Petit Journal

Le Petit Journal
CHAQUE JOUR 5 CENTIMES

Le Supplément illustré
CHAQUE SEMAINE 5 CENTIMES

Huitième année

SUPPLÉMENT ILLUSTRÉ

Huit pages : CINQ centimes

DIMANCHE 28 MARS 1897

ABONNEMENTS

SIX MOIS   UN AN
SEINE ET SEINE-ET-OISE   2 fr.   3 fr. 50
DÉPARTEMENTS   2 fr.   4 fr.
ÉTRANGER   2 50   5 fr.

Numéro 332

UNE NOCE FIN DE SIÈCLE

Wedding on a Bicycle
Henri Meyer
French 1844–1899   Bibliothèque Forney, Paris

Bicycling was a vogue which swept across Europe at the end of the nineteenth century. It appealed particularly to the young. H. G. Wells regarded it as a great emancipating factor. With bicycles, young men and women of modest means living in cities could explore the countryside together in a way which had not been possible before.

The Parisian cyclists in Henri Meyer's picture are clearly well-to-do. So is the old gentleman with the eye-glass, who evidently considers the association of bicycling with marriage as an outrage.

This association is to be found too in the popular English music-hall song of the same period, 'Daisy, Daisy':

> It won't be a stylish marriage,
> I can't afford a carriage,
> But you'd look sweet
> Upon the seat
> Of a bicycle made for two.

Meyer's bride is wearing a long skirt, but the two girls behind her are wearing more practical red bloomers.

The latter were the mid-nineteenth-century invention of an Englishwoman named Amelia Bloomer. They were greeted at the time with general ridicule, but they came into fashion some fifty years later, when long, trailing skirts were found inconvenient for cycling.

The Wedding
Henri Rousseau (Le Douanier Rousseau)
French 1844–1910   Louvre, Paris

Le Douanier Rousseau was, as the name he is generally known by implies, a customs officer. As an artist he was untrained; he defied the laws of composition, yet he achieved fame and success in his lifetime. He is acknowledged today as one of the greatest of modern primitive painters.

In contrast with his style, the people he liked to paint were in no way original. Many of them, indeed, were extremely conventional, and nowhere is this more evident than in this picture of a wedding.

The woman kneeling on the bride's left is probably her grandmother. She clearly admires the bridal dress, and it is quite likely that she made it herself. The dog too is an evident part of a respectable, bourgeois household.

All the members of the group give the impression of having just turned towards a camera to have their photograph taken – a photograph which will be framed and given a place of honour in an overcrowded sitting-room.

Rousseau retired from the customs service in his forties and only then took up painting as a full-time occupation.

The Wedding Meal
Albert-Auguste Fourie

French 1854–1937   Musée des Beaux Arts, Rouen

Fourie was a popular French Realist painter of the late nineteenth and early twentieth century. The bride in his painting is dressed in what is now the traditional manner – in white and with flowers in her hair. The white wedding, as we know it today, originated in the nineteenth century. Before then wedding gowns were elaborate versions of ordinary dresses.

In nineteenth-century France it was assumed that a bride would bring a dowry to her husband. The amount of money involved naturally varied according to the financial standing of the girl's family. In some cases it could amount to a fortune, but even the poorest families tried somehow to find money for a dowry, however modest, or gifts in kind, such as land.

In addition, the bride's parents were expected to provide a trousseau and part of the furniture for the young couple's new home, as well as paying for the wedding.

Bride and Groom
Amedeo Modigliani
Italian 1884–1920   Museum of Modern Art, New York

Modigliani, who first made his reputation as a sculptor, produced his finest paintings in the last five years of his life.

The bride in this picture, with her short-cropped hair, long earrings and exaggerated make-up, is clearly one of the emancipated young women of Modigliani's last years.

This was the period of World War I and its immediate aftermath. During the war, with so many men killed or in the trenches, women took on jobs such as driving ambulances or working in factories which before then would have been considered quite unsuitable.

The elongated lines Modigliani used serve to emphasize a quality of hardness, even slight masculinity, in the newly emancipated woman.

There is usually only one figure in Modigliani's paintings, and this treatment of a newly married couple is a rare exception.

Bride of Christ
Johan Thorn Prikker
Dutch 1868–1932   Rijksmuseum Kroller-Muller, Otterloo

Medieval craftsmen worked in mosaic and stained glass; there have always been some artists who adapted traditional crafts, and Thorn Prikker, well-known for his avant-garde compositions, designed many modern church windows.

The painting of this modern nun, the Bride of Christ, is based on equally traditional symbols. Her white veil suggests purity, she is protected by the outstreched arms of the Christ figure, and his Crown of Thorns becomes a circlet of laurel leaves on her head.

The heavy black lines of the painting may well have been intended as the leading of a glass window, while the stippled background on the right has been drawn from an even earlier tradition of mosaic fresco. All in all, a deeply moving adaptation of a very ancient image.

Bride and Bridegroom
Wassily Kandinsky
Russian 1866–1944   Staatliche Galerie, Munich

Kandinsky gave up a promising legal career in Moscow to study painting in Munich. He soon became a leading figure in modern art and is generally acknowledged to have been the first serious artist to paint a purely abstract picture, i.e. one without any recognizable subject.

Kandinsky believed that, just as in music sounds can conjure up images, so in painting colours can achieve the same effects. A strong red, for example, could produce an effect similar to that of a musical fortissimo.

There was, however, a phase in Kandinsky's career when he painted figurative pictures with an almost medieval quality. The *Bride and Bridegroom* is from this period. It is interesting that such an avant-garde painter should have chosen to present the bride held protectively in the bridegroom's arms in a setting as romantic as any painter's imagination could conjure up.

The Country Wedding
Grandma Moses (Anna Mary Robertson Moses)
American 1860–1961   Private Collection

In earlier times American couples were often married in the home of the bride, a practice which immigrants brought with them from England. In fine weather the reception commonly took place out of doors.

A country wedding was a subject which naturally appealed to the extraordinary artist known as Grandma Moses, who began painting at the age of seventy-eight.

'If I didn't start painting,' she wrote in her autobiography, 'I would have raised chickens.' Of her own technique she wrote:

'Before I start painting I get a frame, then I saw my masonite board to fit the frame. (I always thought it a good idea to build the sty before getting the pig, likewise with young men, get the home before the wedding.)'

She sold her first picture through her local drugstore but, before long, she had fifteen one-woman shows in the United States and Europe.

Registry Office
Norman Rockwell

American 1894–1978   The Norman Rockwell Foundation

Norman Rockwell wrote in his autobiography: 'I do ordinary people in everyday situations and that's about all I can do.'

It was a fair description of his work, even if it suggests an over-modest assessment of his achievement.

The picture of the registry office presents a scene which could have been duplicated in hundreds of small American towns.

The bright yellow dress of the pretty girl makes her the focal point of the picture. The sincerity and love of the young couple are beyond all doubt.

The painting was originally created for the cover of *Saturday Evening Post* magazine, for which Rockwell produced numerous pictures. A collection of them would be a revealing record of American life in his time.

Among the subjects he treated were people in a barber's shop, a woman and her grandson saying grace in a railway restaurant, and the first walk on the moon.

Rockwell had humour and a strong narrative sense, both of which emerge clearly in his paintings. He has been described as the artist who better than any other protrayed the American dream, and it is surely this above all which explains his exceptional popularity in the United States.

Sources

Greek Vase Painting
British Museum, London

The Aldobrandini Wedding
Vatican Library, Rome

GIOTTO: *Marriage at Cana*
Arena Chapel, Padua

HEILIGENKREUTZ: *The Mystical Marriage of St Catherine*
Kunsthistoriches Museum, Vienna

VAN EYCK: *The Arnolfini Wedding*
National Gallery, London

FOUQUET: *The Marriage of the Virgin*
Musée Condé, Chantilly (Giraudon)

CRANACH: *Princess Sibylle of Cleve as Bride*
Schlossmuseum, Weimar

BRUEGHEL: *The Peasant Wedding*
Kunsthistoriches Museum, Vienna (Bridgeman)

RUBENS: *Marriage of Marie de' Medici to Henry IV*
Louvre, Paris (Bridgeman)

REMBRANDT: *The Jewish Wedding*
Rijksmuseum, Amsterdam (Bridgeman)

UTAMARO: *A Courtesan Dreaming of Her Wedding*
British Museum, London

GOYA: *The Wedding*
Museo Nacional del Prado, Madrid (Arxiu Mas)

LAMI: *Fête at the Château de Versailles on the Occasion of the Marriage of the Dauphin in 1745*
Victoria and Albert Museum, London (Bridgeman)

FRITH: *The Wedding of the Prince of Wales and Princess Alexandra*
Royal Collection, London

MEYER: *Wedding on a Bicycle*
Bibliothèque Forney, Paris (Bridgeman)

ROUSSEAU: *The Wedding*
Musée Nationaux, Paris (Bridgeman)

FOURIE: *The Wedding Meal*
Musée des Beaux-Arts, Rouen

MODIGLIANI: *Bride and Groom*
Museum of Modern Art, New York

PRIKKER: *Bride of Christ*
Rijksmuseum Kroller-Muller, Otterloo (Bridgeman)

KANDINSKY: *Bride and Bridegroom*
Staatliche Galerie, Munich

MOSES: *The Country Wedding*
Galerie St Etienne, New York

ROCKWELL: *Registry Office*
The Norman Rockwell Foundation